POETIC TALES OF A TRAVELLING GIRL

To Caroline and Allan,

I hope you enjoy
reading this,

Emma Ross.

Published by

Librario Publishing Ltd

ISBN: 1-904440-79-7

Copies can be ordered via the Internet
www.librario.com

or from:

Brough House, Milton Brodie, Kinloss
Moray IV36 2UA
Tel /Fax No 00 44 (0)1343 850 617

Printed and bound by Digisource GB Ltd

'The world isn't just the way it is. It is how we understand it, no? And in understanding something, we bring something to it, no? Doesn't that make life a story?' - *Life of Pi*.

How would you tell yours?

Everyone has a story, a history. There is no one truth, no one coherent universal experience of something. Life is just a web of tangled experiences, different stories – conflicting, varying, multiple versions of events – that collide and smash and exist together. And so it is with this in mind that I write this now: this is my truth, my own story, my understanding. Just another voice from the polyphonic depths of a world filled with interwoven stories and myths. This is a collection of moments, recorded in fragments of poetry, journal entries and photographs. Fragmented memories that circle and surface in no chronological order, flooding back in disjointed waves. I will never forget the journey and I collect these moments together here for anyone and everyone, but mostly for myself so that I never lose sight of the person I became.

People always ask you where you're going, where you're headed, what your plans are, both in travelling and in life in general. They often expect you to know exactly in which direction you're moving but what if your plan is to have no plan? Travelling taught me many things including to live in the moment, to move from place to place on an 'I'll-see-what-happens-when-I-arrive' basis. Because, as my father used to sing, 'you never know where you're going until you get there'. My journey, my story, is a validation of that very idea; I never did know where I was going but it always seemed to be irrelevant. The journey, and not the destination, is what really seemed to matter. And it was the people that I met who made the journey what it was. This is for you all. It is merely an attempt to convey the experience of travelling and I hope that everyone can feel the way I did. Thanks to those who showed me around their country and to those who explored it with me – I'm so glad that our paths crossed. A special thank you to you, Candice.

'It's all about the journey'.

First Flight

Bright blue
Fading into a hazy glowing red
Clouds laced in amber streaks
Point to where the sun fled seconds before
Setting the horizon on fire.
The sky burns on as I look on
And the torched edges of the endless blue
Grow dark at the end of the evening song
In the long pause before the weary moon
Washes away the colours and bathes the heavens in darkness.

5th October 2004, Taiwan

THE DREAM

I stood at the edge of the world and thought about taking flight. A crowd of people stood behind me; some sceptical, some encouraging, most with some disbelief written on their face. I stepped closer but instead of thinking about the enormity of what was ahead I watched the sun rise – stretching into a powdered red sky, sleepily rising out of a bed of clouds. I drank in the simple beauty of the morning and without another thought or glance behind me, I jumped. The world as I knew it spun away and I flew. And I flew. That leap into the unknown was the day that my ordinary world changed forever; the day I boarded a plane and didn't look back.

RÉN SHÁN RÉN HǍI
'PEOPLE MOUNTAIN, PEOPLE SEA'

I feel like I'm being shaken awake
Senses bombarded
By different things clinging to me all at once.
My eyes seem to open for the first time
And every time I blink
Something new hits me
I blink
And my world spins into one
That's stuck in traffic
I blink
And my world's been exchanged
For the glare of a neon sign
I blink
And I'm in another crowd
Facing the wrong way.
I blink
And there are dragons in the skyscrapers
That turn around and wink.

6th October 2004, Taiwan

I sat in awe today as the world of Taipei flew past in a haze of smoke, motorbikes and crowds... 'people mountain people sea' is a exactly how it feels when you first arrive: as if you are being pulled along into an endless sea of people. Unable to fight the current you lose yourself in the chaotic crowds that move in tides and it is this feeling that is initially so overwhelming. Yet it is the very same feeling I welcomed. I sat there trying to take in the streams of traffic, the shouting, the huge skyscrapers and neon signs everywhere... I love being somewhere so full of life, so different to anything I've experienced before.

THE TURTLE AND THE BIRD

Hidden amongst the sea of green
Five red posts hold up an ornate roof
Proudly exhibiting the sloping tiles
That return at the end to face heaven.
And all around hundreds of leafy stalks
Stretch up in adoration to the sun
Bending in the breeze in prayer
And nodding appreciation for the light.

A turtle glides slowly
In a mist of water
Diving down and re-surfacing
In a mirrored reflection of the bird.

I took the tube to Chiang-Kai Shek Memorial Hall this afternoon and walked to the Botanical Gardens. It was lovely there; I sat I just sat by a bridge for a while, thinking about everything and nothing at all. Sitting on a bench in the sun near a lotus pond I wrote this:

On a rock in the middle of the pond a white and grey bird stands proudly, fixing beady eyes on one spot before something else catches his gaze. A turtle slowly climbs out of the water and pulls himself with some difficulty onto the same rock, lifting his head to stare straight up at the bird. I watch with a smile creeping across my face: the bird looks down and they stay like that for a short time, with the turtle and the bird staring at each other, inches apart. They appear, from here, to be deep in conversation.

Shortly after the turtle slides back into the water and disappears. Presumably to report back to the fish.

JUXTAPOSITION

Old meets new
In a collision of colour
Old merges with new
In an extension of itself.
The contemporary circles tradition
And snakes out of the past
But they do not clash.
One grows out of the other;
Learning, adapting, adding
And moving on as boundaries blur
In a challenge to the world of boxes
This city is living, breathing art.

This morning I went to the Museum of Contemporary Art and saw an exhibition called 'Fiction.Love'. It was so interesting; exploring the aesthetics of the comic book in Asia's popular culture and I enjoyed studying this 'merging of digitalised images and art'. It hit me at this modern exhibition that after looking at so much traditional ink work and calligraphy recently that it was almost a reflection of the city as a whole – a place where the contemporary and the traditional are continually juxtaposed. It is like finding a beautiful temple standing defiantly amongst the skyscrapers.

The Enlightened One

In the last flicker of light
I find you.
You are unsmiling and move slowly
You watch the steady stream of people
Without comment, but with interest
You do not judge me,
Quietly regarding me with curiosity.
You show me the simplicity of your life
Without a word.
Your eyes, too, are unspeaking,
For in them lies the secret for which we search.

The light fades as the carp disappears
With a quick flick of the tail
But his whiskers twitch in a slight smile of knowing.

I am at Longshan Temple (Longshan means 'dragon mountain') which was built in 1738. Outside the streets are teeming with people, numerous stands sell pink flowers and prayer beads. I can hardly get through the crowds. The entrance gates lead to a courtyard which has three waterfalls on the right hand side. Whiskered carp swim in the pools underneath, creating a swirling pattern of red, white and orange. I watch them for a while and then turn to the temple, so colourful and intricate. Two patterned red paper balloons hang on either side of the main door… the roof is a bright mix of dragons, birds and other carefully carved figures. There is so much to see, smell and hear my senses seem over loaded all at once. I enter the side door where people are spilling out, and I am hit by a cloud of incense which makes the air heavy with its smoke. I'm trying to remember every detail as I look around; there are decorative pillars where I'm standing and in front seems to be the central courtyard where large tables are covered with fruit and flowers, like some sort of offering. Through the haze of incense I can see the main temple room in front of which people are bowing, kneeling, talking quietly; the gesture of prayer shows me that some things easily transcend language barriers.

SPEECHLESS

Don't understand what's going on
I'm deaf and blind in this world without text.
I'm lost to the shouts
And letters flashing warnings in red,
Passing me by
Unseen and unheard,
Flying over my head.
Adrift among crowds
I wonder whether to turn and run
Or wait for the explanation
I won't understand.

15th October 2004, Taiwan

An earthquake hit today. And somehow I didn't even feel it. I was in Taipei Main Station when it happened, working out flights to Hong Kong, and when I headed down to catch a tube to Xindian I noticed all of the escalators had been shut down. As I went further underground I became aware of large numbers of people standing and sitting around, which struck me as unusual in a place where they are usually rushing past in streams, and that the platforms were empty. I quickly realised that there were policemen beside the closed gates and my first thought was that there had been a bomb scare. The screens with travel details had been replaced with red flashing symbols in Chinese and, blocked by an unyielding language barrier, I had absolutely no idea what had happened, walking around in complete confusion. It wasn't until this evening that I found out an earthquake had hit 7 on the Richter Scale out at sea and 4 in Taiwan. My first experience of an earthquake and I was oblivious to it all.

KIDNAPPED

Steal me away tonight
When time falls asleep
Just take me from here
Please take me to where I can hide.
Just steal me tonight
And keep me when light dies
I'll hide in your eyes
And the world will be quiet again.
Or steal him for me
Bring him here as it all disappears
Hold me and hide me
From all that is lost
And all that is new won't pass by.

Travelling makes you realise that you are one speck on a massive surface. The world that you knew previously is stretched and extended until you realise how small it had been and how huge it can be. How many millions of stories there are, and histories and thoughts and languages and beliefs and ideas and religions all circulating out there. And you are simply an unknown foreigner, sitting writing in a notebook as all these things continue to go on around you. And how they have always been doing so without you sitting there. There is so much to see and explore in this world it is almost impossible to fathom. So many opportunities right there before you. And having travelled hundreds of miles, gotten lost in a new world – so different from anything I have known before – I realise that this is just the tiniest fraction of it; there are still vast and endless numbers of experiences waiting.

Elevated

Lost to time, hidden behind a cloud
There is a forgotten place
Misplaced when the months ran away with the days,
Locked high in the mountain
Where the sun falls
That's what they say.
We can go there, you and I,
To find the river
And follow it to yesterday
And hide there, in the sky.
We'll stay there, watching time slide by,
Until tomorrow passes and forgets us
And we too are lost to time
Hidden behind a cloud.

17th October 2004, Taiwan

I have just climbed Xianji Rock at Jingmei and I cannot find the words to describe it. Even trying to do so feels like some act of betrayal to its silent beauty. It quite simply stuns me and there is nothing in my mind apart from the desperate attempt to remember the detail of the sun setting over the mountains. I sit in a wooden hut looking out on Taipei as day quietly surrenders to dusk. A man in front of me is stretching and doing t'ai chi whilst another sings a refrain in Chinese. Apart from this and the distant noises of the city I can hear only birds. To my right is a brightly coloured dragon which crawls in stone over the roof of a temple. I sit still in the dying sunlight, in this veiled world above the city.

I try to remember it all –
The sound, every sight,
The smell of walking through the market late last night.
So you can sleep with the sun
As it fades from the blushing sky
And feel the air pushing through
in a world that's rushing by.
(Can you see it through my eyes?)
So you know why I try to freeze this frame
and keep it underneath my skin,
To live in me,
To stop the world from spinning
As I replay the memory.

18th October 2004, Taiwan

Whilst I was walking this afternoon I realised what makes it such an experience to be wandering on the streets of Taipei: there is so much colour around, and you are constantly hit by a different sound, sight and smell with every single step. And you never know what you'll find around the next corner. I walked along, meandering up and down the streets, taking it all in and walked home lost in the crowds and in my thoughts.

FAITH

I swam into your eyes
When you pushed me over the clouds
I ran into the tide and was swept into your smile
When you surfaced in my life.
And like the promise that is born
Every morning with the sunrise
And hangs behind the afternoon waiting,
You are there as constant
As the dawn is breaking.

19th October 2004, Taiwan

Today I went to the National Palace Museum and saw some really interesting exhibitions. I particularly enjoyed 'The Art and Aesthetics of Form: Selections from the History of Chinese Painting' and 'A Picture is Worth More than a Thousand Words'. The art work was incredible and I took a few notes during a video:

'The collaboration of painting, calligraphy and poetry is unique to Chinese art; some artists feel a poetic phrase conveys a more complete message.'

'The poetry and painting reinforce and compliment one another … *In painting there is poetry and in poetry there is painting*'.

K'GARI

I listen to her poems in the night
When her shadow slips into the sea
And the wet sand is lit up with a line of green stars
Especially for the moon.
I hear her verses
When the stars are shooting by
And the world wakes up with red eyes
To the birth of colour on the dunes.
I listen to her poetry as waves are crashing
Over my head
And I breathe in the beauty of the day
Before it fades away and I exhale.
I listen to her poems as the sands move and the breeze
Makes the world dance
As the endless sky throws me into a daze
And she is always writing, and her world is strewn with verse
For she is the land,
And the greatest poet.

I left this morning for a three day tour of Fraser Island. We drove to Rainbow Beach and then boarded a ferry, which only took five minutes to make the crossing over to the island. It is absolutely breathtaking here. I especially enjoyed climbing sand dunes today and then sand boarding back down. This evening when I was lying on the dunes counting shooting stars I lay thinking how beautiful this world is – and that the beauty is as fleeting as one of the stars and as old and enduring as the weathered sand that colours the cliffs. It really is an island of poetry; verses are submerged in dunes and float under the water, pass in the sky and lie in the footsteps.

The Artist

A whirlwind of colours
Creates and recreates the skies-
Moulding, hitting, raining, staining
Coming into the blue.
A watered rainbow,
A hurricane,
The reflection of a rainbow hurricane
Circling the sun.
Spirals in the breeze and splashes on stone,
The whirlwind that crashes by
Leaves nothing untouched.
Sunlight hits water and blurs this image
Through eyes brimming over with
The rain of colours in the wind.

She is his muse
And he sees her everywhere.

This place is amazing. We drove to a lake this morning which was like a cup of tea – the water was coloured a surprising array of deep red, orange, brown and yellow (to do with trees disintegrating into the water). It was a perched lake – a body of water in a sand dune formed because the 'coffee rock' has created a base for the lake. We swam and took pictures of its fantastic colours. The second lake was equally beautiful but was by contrast a clear turquoise that met with dark blue. I felt so lucky to be seeing all of this and wanted to hold onto every second of today.

UNCONDITIONALLY

When the sky falls down I'll sing to you.
When the water's dry I'll swim to you.
When day is night and dark is light,
I'll win the fight and be with you.

When worlds are spinning I'll dance with you.
When the end is beginning I'll cry for you.
When fire grows cold and nothing grows old,
I'll ignore all I'm told and stay with you.

When time's slipping backwards I'll be there with you.
When words lose their meaning I'll keep speaking to you
When I open my eyes and the moon passes by,
I'll sleep in the sky and keep running to you.

'It must be amazing to have this as your job,' I said to Keith, our tour guide, 'to show people this place that you love'. He looked at me and his expression said before he did, 'What is the point in doing something you *don't* love?'

My conversation with him on the way back from Fraser Island really made me think. He is so passionate about the island, which is evident not only in the way that he talks about it, but also in his photography of it. Here I am, travelling across the world in search of answers (what will I do with my life?) and it's so clear to him – do what you love and live your life. There's little point in anything else. He commented on society's need to define a person's value by what they do, and said his ex-girlfriend has been travelling for a year and a half , changing from one job to the next but 'just living and being happy'. He also talked about how travelling changes a person, and I know that my thinking and views have been altered from all of these experiences. I've learnt so much even in this three-day trip, some things I didn't even know about myself. I noticed before we left this morning that this was written on the wall:

'Just keep walking. The earth is big and life is short.'

Unanswered

Is it wrong to miss you?
Are you thinking of me?
Will you sail over mountains
And swim through the skies
To reach me tonight?
Will it be the same, can we keep how it was then
Now and know that it's not?
Will it will I can we should you
Might I won't you must I could you
Can it don't you won't we must you
Damn it can't I want to keep you?
Questions fall silent, unanswered
You don't belong to me, you don't,
You live in a borrowed dream.

I had a conversation with Jenaya today about meeting people for a reason. Since I've been travelling it is something that I have thought a lot about – was I destined to meet certain people at certain times or did our paths cross by some coincidence? We talked about the effect that meeting someone can have on your life; whether it's someone you talk to at the bar for five minutes or someone you've known for a few months. The book I'm reading just now, *The Five People You Meet in Heaven* by Mitch Albom, also explores this idea: your life is explained to you by five people who were in it, 'these people may have been loved ones or distant strangers. Yet each of them changed your path forever'. Even the briefest of meetings can change your life, even in the smallest way. 'It is because the human spirit knows, deep down, that all lives intersect... we think such things are random. But there is a balance to it all.'

ISLAND LIFE

I lost myself along the way
But you'll find me on the road someday
Where the palm trees pattern the sky.
You'll find me in a hammock under a yellow moon
On the sand by the edge of the world
Watching it sail by.
You'll hear me when the sun weeps and the clouds burn
You'll see me with a white flower in my hair
Running when there's nothing more to learn.
You'll see me as the ocean tips
And throws me back again,
You'll find me someday
When I've circled the sea
You'll find me when I've learnt to be.

28th November 2004, Queensland, Australia

I'm writing this as I lie in a hammock on the beach. I feel unbelievably relaxed – looking up I see palm trees and a cloudless sky, to the right is a gorgeous stretch of green-blue ocean and the hills of the mainland in the distance. I've just woken up after falling asleep in the sun, swaying in the wind. I love working in the bar here; the people are so friendly, the view is amazing and the weather is beautiful. I still can't quite believe I've ended up living on a tropical island on the edge of the Great Barrier Reef …

And I feel really lucky to have met so many great friends here. For the second time this year, summer has just begun.

STOWAWAY

Worlds apart
On different lands, different tides
Crash on different shores
Yet I still feel pulled to you and yours.
You hold me in an unrelenting grip
When you look at me
And I'm afraid of all that means.
You may be there but I seem to have carried you with me
In these thoughts of you
And accidentally let you keep this hold on me
And there's nothing I can do
So don't release me;
Let the tides carry me home
If it's you I'm meant to see.

New Year's Eve was fantastic … when I finished work we sat down on the beach until sunrise. I looked round at one point and hundreds of people were all standing on the decking facing the mainland as the first sun of 2005 sleepily began to rise. … I'm getting sad about leaving Magnetic Island now – I will miss my Island in the Sun. I underlined a page of the book I'm reading at the moment as it seemed to stand out at me:

'I guess that's all forever is,' his father replied. 'Just one long trail of nows. And I guess all you can do is try and live one now at a time without getting too worked up about the next now.' And that was all she would live and breathe and think of, Annie resolved, nothing beyond nor nothing past… One protracted moment along the trail of nows…And whatever came to pass …this moment would be there, indelibly written in their heads and hearts forever.' ~ *The Horse Whisperer.*

Before Parting

Our paths crossed for a moment in time
I was yours and you were mine
And that new day was ours.
We painted the sky with our words
As the world was waking
And it was only for us that the dawn was breaking,
There was no one but us in the world.
And I was yours completely
There was nothing but your smile
And as the sky faded out of sight
We fought over the colour of the clouds
In the disappearing light
And I held you and was held by you
And was yours alone for that night.

Being a backpacker is so much more than travelling with luggage on your back. It is a mindset; life is simplified. The things that used to matter seem insignificant in comparison to the world that has been rolled out before you. It is the most freeing way to travel; for a while your life consists of sunrises and beaches, airports and hostels, strangers and friends who were strangers only a day earlier. You become stronger, more willing to try the things that used to fill you with fear. Somewhere, if it wasn't already there, the desire for adventure has seeped into your skin and every day starts with the realisation of endless possibility. It is an education like no other. You are challenged constantly, your eyes and mind are opened and you are filled with a growing need to learn, see and experience more.

'You have to take risks, he said. We will only understand the miracle of life fully when we allow the unexpected to happen.'

~ Paulo Coelho, *By the River Piedra I Sat Down and Wept*

A World on Pause

Freeze today
So I can remain this way a little longer.
Just press pause and I'll hold onto this moment
With both hands
Just press pause and I'll lie here
In the broken remnants of morning
And be with you
As if it will always be this way
Don't let me freefall back into the way
It has to be
Please just freeze today.

Snow covered mountains rise out of the body of water that lies flat below me. I sit on a frost- covered bench, my cheeks red from the cold and the walk. I'm climbing Mount Iron to get an aerial view of Wanaka. It's a beautiful morning. The journey down from Franz Josef yesterday was as incredible as everyone had promised. But perhaps I fail as an English Literature student in my complete inability to describe the scenery and its effect on me. I feel like the sun floods into my soul and there is a lightness in my heart. That the day breaks just for me every morning. Words are just not adequate; they fall short when I want to explain how the light catches the tops of the mountains, and the way they reflect in the water. Perhaps it is enough just to say that the smile in my eyes is a reflection of the uncontrollable laughter in my soul.

FREEFALL

Will you catch me if I fall?
If it all collapses tomorrow,
And I land on yesterday
Will you catch me if I fall?
If I walk across the clouds
And over the edge of the bay
Will you catch me if I fall?
If I'm sinking fast and the world is slipping by
And it's spinning past as I dive through the sky
Would you catch me at all?

20th June 2005, New Zealand

I just jumped out of a plane! I can't believe I actually did it – me! I checked in last night to Go Global Backpackers in Taupo where a very helpful guy talked about things to do here. I showed an interest in skydiving and before I knew it I had provisionally agreed to do the jump. He promised it was going to be sunny today and a perfect day for throwing yourself out of an aircraft. True to his word I woke up this morning to him knocking on the door saying I was booked to do a 12,000 foot jump at 11.30am. Oh. Dear. Lord.

I was really nervous all morning but there was little time to think about it all – we got changed into jumpsuits, harnessed and filmed so that our fear was well documented and we were shown how our arms and legs should be positioned on leaving the aircraft. All this was done in a flash and then suddenly we were in the plane and climbing up into a piercing blue sky. The guy at the hostel was right – it was a great day with spectacular views over Lake Taupo. My instructor strapped himself to me (as I double checked we were indeed attached) and it felt so surreal, I don't think I realised what I was doing.

I'm admiring the view when suddenly my goggles are on, we're edging closer to the door which flies open and then we're falling falling falling and everything is spinning, it's incredible, I can't scream (I can barely breathe), I close my eyes, the sound of air rushing past fills my ears falling falling falling and I open my eyes and quickly close them and I can't think I just fall. Suddenly I'm jolted back and the parachute opens and then slowly there is silence. And all is calm. It is truly amazing. He takes off my goggles and we quietly sail down, and there is so much emotion inside of me that I don't know how to react. I just look around in wonder. Here I am, in the middle of the sky – right out in the middle of the sky! The world below is still spinning, my stomach is lurching and I still can't believe it is happening. Terror is replaced with awe. And suddenly I never want this to end, I feel so alive; excitement and freedom and disbelief all flooding me in waves and all I can do is hang on and gaze around at the world which is fast approaching. And then my feet hit the floor and we have landed. It's over so fast, too fast and it all disappears so quickly as I try to replay it and relive it. I cannot stop smiling as I look up and see how far I have just come.

This was written on a flyer and caught my eye:
'Why jump out of a perfectly good aeroplane? ... deep in the human consciousness is a pervasive need for a logical universe that makes sense. But the real universe is always one step beyond logic. We do these' things. It is something deep within us... it is the spirit of man....Embrace the fear'.

INTERSECTIONS

I don't know when I'll find you
But I know I will
I don't know how I'll lose you
Once I'm in your arms again
But I know you'll make me go
And maybe if it's meant to be
You'll take me back
To our beginning
And begin again with me.

47

Isn't it strange how two people can be together for so long, their worlds intertwined and their paths running alongside each other and then suddenly one of them veers to the side? We are all worlds spinning separately and suddenly one world breaks off, continues in another direction and then just as suddenly collides with another. Is it down to chance? Or are we always set on this collision course towards each other? Perhaps, like the idea in Paulo Coelho's *Eleven Minutes*, in a world of chance encounters, coincidences, and randomness there is a thread underlying it all and weaving it together. Perhaps people are set on different paths at different stages in their lives at a time when their path will cross with another's at an exact moment. At that point, when you look up and meet someone else's glance, there in that second, two worlds have spun and crashed. What a thought …. One brief smile, one glance and one life can be forever altered. And it's true; you walk in and out of people's lives, changed that little bit every time from the impact of having met each other.

.

Mirrored	Mirrored
I'm	I'm
looking back	back looking
my past	past my
world	world
disappears yours and	and yours disappears
mine	mine
yours is	is yours
mine	mine
just being	being just
your	your
reverse	reverse

49

Milford Sound is just breathtaking. It looks like something from the Jurassic period; a valley carved out by a glacier. We went on a river cruise for 2 hours and it rained a bit but the clouds and fog only added to its mysterious atmosphere. The clouds were so low that they literally hovered above the water. And dolphins swam alongside the boat, gracefully following us for a while, making it even more spectacular. The whole place just captivated me. Stopped at a few places on the way back to take photos – one was a beautiful mirror lake reflecting the snowy mountains.

RETROSPECTION

Frozen images
Break apart in my mind
Jagged snapshots
Rewind to begin again.
Discarded shards of memory,
Scattered in a sea of meaning
And trapped in a bottle beneath the waves.

8th June 2005, Western Australia

I'm in Coral Bay and have had such a fantastic day, I think this may be my favourite place in Australia. Donna and I went on a snorkelling/ kayak tour – there were three kayaks in the group and it was hard going but a great feeling. We went out for about ten minutes and put on flippers and snorkel masks (without much ease in such a small space) and jumped into the water. It was absolutely breathtaking. I felt like I was part of the school of blue fish that were all around me; I turned and dove and circled and felt like we were in some sort of dance. It was so pretty. We reluctantly pulled ourselves back into the kayaks and continued on for another ten minutes of hard paddling. The coral here was great and we saw a huge turtle within minutes. It didn't seem to mind six people tailing it and glided along unfazed. One of my favourite things about this spot was swimming over what looked like a coral wall and suddenly passing over the edge and seeing the colours change with the drop … It really was like entering another, silent and peaceful, world.

THROUGH THE WINDOW

Hills slope into hills
Slope into hills
Disappear into a sinking sky
Heavy blanket falling
Landing on nothing but stillness
Shafts of light rip the creases of cloud
Tearing through the blue sky
And slipping underneath.

Today was a beautiful day for travelling – blue skies and amazing scenery. The drive from the West Coast to Queenstown to Christchurch has been spectacular, definitely the best journey so far. I sat next to an elderly lady who was on her way to see her grandchildren and she entertained me with stories of her family (she had been with her husband since she was 16 years old!). Going through valleys by the coast and watching the rolling mountains fall into the sea, travelling inland and seeing the magnificent Mount Cook rise out of the hills…it was stunning. Apparently I was lucky to see it as it's normally covered in cloud (its Maori name is 'cloud piercer'). Seeing the turquoise green Lake Tekapo with Mount Cook in the background was just amazing. Yet again I struggle to convey the true beauty of the moment – the kind of beauty that hits you hard. Words are just words – breathtaking, beautiful, striking that seem meaningless when you are confronted by such a view.

COMPANIONSHIP

Every morning I wake and find you here
You have not fallen through that space
Or disappeared through the hole
Where dreams meet the real.
The night has not stolen you,
For you are not hers to steal.
You lie with an arm slung sleepily across me
And a new morning watches us stir
As a new song is sung
We kiss in our sleep
And the day has begun.

I live in your smile
I breathe in your gaze
And I am held in the laughter
That lights every day.

11th June 2005, Western Australia

Three people sit watching the sun set. They do not speak and are comfortable in the silence. Dark grey clouds trail across the stretch of blue and the silhouettes of two people fishing in the bay become the general point of gaze. They have spent four days in each other's company and they sit together on their last evening, each absorbed in their own thoughts. They are all at different stages in their lives and somehow their different searches and directions have meant that their lives have all intersected here. After the sun has set and the bay is flooded with darkness, they begin again on their separate journeys, but each taking something from the encounter.

MEETING PLACE

Hold me in your arms
One last time
Before the train wrenches me from your embrace,
From this bittersweet place,
Where happiness shifts into melancholy
As quickly as doors open and close.
Months filled with elation and deflation,
As I arrive and leave,
Leave and retrieve
The last embrace.
And you're there waiting for me
As endless as the dream
That forever holds this smile in place.

26th July 2005, Queensland, Australia

It doesn't get any easier, saying goodbye. That's the thing about travelling – you meet so many amazing people and you know you have to part but it never gets any easier. So in the end you just have to enjoy the time you have together, no matter how long it lasts. And you never know when you may meet again.

And now here I sit, digging my toes into the sand and listening to Jack Johnson, with thoughts of the goodbyes I've made recently. I have one week left in Australia – this time next week I'll be boarding a plane for Taiwan. It hasn't hit me yet, I can't imagine actually flying home. Ten months on and I don't feel anything like the girl who left home. I sit with images and memories from my travels flash flooding around me: from standing on a surf board to throwing myself out of a plane in Taupo (my ultimate, and literal, leap of faith), from flying over the Twelve Apostles in a helicopter with Candice to climbing a glacier in New Zealand, from scuba diving to cart wheeling along a white sand beach to having conversations through the night until sunrise... I smile as I flip through the photo album of my mind, reliving the trip – my first attempt to embrace life and all the adventure it offers.

THIS EVENING

This evening, the sky was set alight
As I walked into the horizon,
Tripping on the single thread
Hemming line to line.
This evening, the sun lost its grip on the day
As embers flicker and fade
And footsteps run into the waves.
I can't see when or where it changed
It's all been rearranged so many times before.
And now I'm here again, walking on the shore
Listening to a song on repeat
A song on repeat
And I find myself where I lost myself before.

27th July 2005, Queensland, Australia

And so I walked away and didn't turn back. I looked only at the stretch of beach in front of me. I liked to think that there was something symbolic about having left my name etched into the sand. I smiled at the thought that had just occurred to me about travelling – you always leave your mark on the places you've been – a memory that someone else will laugh at, a lasting imprint on someone else's life… and that really is the most special thing about travelling.

Movements of the Tide

I stand here now
As my mother before me
And hers before her –
A verse in an endless song.
I stand here looking at the same sky
Dissolving quietly into an amber soaked sea,
From where the sun will burst through relentlessly
In a trail of tomorrows.
I stand here, like those before and after me,
This generation like the tide,
Following a trail of todays.
I stand here watching, as time walks slowly across the sand
Leaving his mark on an ever-changing land.
For I am just a pebble on the shore.

And I stand at the beginning and end of it all.

7th August 2005, Taiwan

I have learnt so much since that morning I wrote in my first journal in Edinburgh airport. I have changed so much, and grown and had experiences I never even dreamed of. I have made some close friends, I have discovered different parts of me, I have flown, I have landed, I have leapt into the unknown, and I have walked. And kept on walking. Now as I head home I smile at the thought of it all, and hope I never forget the person I have become.

And so it ends. And so it begins.

'It's there in the excitement of the unexpected, in the desire to do something with real fervour, in the certainty that one is going to realise a dream… Passion sends us signals that guide us through our lives and it is up to us to interpret those signs.'

~ Paulo Coelho, *Eleven Minutes*

Layout: latouveilhe@mac.com

Font: Adobe Garamond (11pt)

Copies of this book can be ordered via the Internet:

www.librario.com

or from:

Librario Publishing Ltd
Brough House
Milton Brodie
Kinloss
Moray IV36 2UA
Tel /Fax No 01343 850 617